W9-CCQ-312

BE SAFE ON YOUR BIKE

BRIDGET HEOS   ILLUSTRATED BY SILVIA BARONCELLI

Amicus Illustrated is published by Amicus
P.O. Box 1329, Mankato, MN 56002
www.amicuspublishing.us

Library of Congress Cataloging-in-Publication Data
Heos, Bridget.
 Be safe on your bike / by Bridget Heos, Silvia Baroncelli.
    pages cm. — (Be safe!)
 Includes bibliographical references.
 Summary: "Samantha teaches her somewhat clueless neighbor
boy Jake how to ride his bicycle safely they go for a bike ride
and get ice cream"— Provided by publisher.
 ISBN 978-1-60753-443-3 (library binding) —
ISBN 978-1-60753-658-1 (ebook)
1. Bicycles—Safety measures–Juvenile literature. I. Baroncelli,
Silvia illustrator. II. Title.
 GV1055.H45 2015
 796.6028'9—dc23   2013032363

Editor: Rebecca Glaser
Designer: Kathleen Petelinsek

Printed in the United States of America,
at Corporate Graphics in North Mankato, Minn.
10 9 8 7 6 5 4 3 2 1

ABOUT THE AUTHOR

Bridget Heos is the author of more than
60 children's books, including many
advice and how-to titles. She lives safely
in Kansas City with her husband and four
children. You can find out more about her
at www.authorbridgetheos.com.

ABOUT THE ILLUSTRATOR

Silvia Baroncelli has loved to draw since she
was a child. She collaborates regularly with
publishers in drawing and graphic design from
her home in Prato, Italy. Her best collaborators
are her four nephews, daughter Ginevra, and
organized husband Tommaso. Find out more
about her on the web at silviabaroncelli.it

"Hi Jake! You got a bike? Cool!"
"Mind if I ride with you, Samantha?"
"Where's your helmet?"

3

"Not that kind. It needs to be a bike helmet. And it needs to fit you correctly."

Bike helmets prevent head injuries. And in many places, it's the law to wear one.

"Now. Make sure your bike is ready. Tires pumped? Check. Seat at the right height? Check. Wait a second," Samantha says.

"Jake, why are you barefoot?"

"Um . . ."

"Listen, you have to wear shoes while riding a bike. Otherwise, you can hurt your feet really badly."

"Hold on. That's not a very good idea. You need both hands free to steer the bike."

"And I know you're not going to text and ride!
Where did you even get that cell phone?"

"I was just borrowing it, bro!" Jake says.

"Now we're ready. Let's ride on the sidewalk until we get to the bike trail. Watch out for walkers."

"You can't just *watch* the walkers. You have to go around them. Pedestrians have the right-of-way on the sidewalk."

"Uh-oh. The bike trail has a big hill. Do you know what to do?"

"Jake, don't close your eyes! Genlly push on your brakes to slow down. That way, you won't lose control. If the hill is too steep, get off your bike and walk."

"Where should we go?"

"How about ice cream?"

Bike riding is fun. Just be sure
to get where you're going safely.

BIKE SAFETY RULES TO REMEMBER

- For riders age 10 and under, it's safest to ride on the sidewalk or bike trails.
- Watch for dogs, objects left on the sidewalk, crooked and bumpy sidewalks, and other hazards that could make you crash.
- Bicyclists older than 10 should learn traffic rules before riding in the street.
- It's safest to ride during the day instead of at night.
- Have your parents make sure your helmet fits and meets safety standards.

GLOSSARY WORDS

hazard An unsafe object that you need to go around.

head injury Physical harm to the scalp, skull or brain.

helmet A protective head piece.

law A rule created by the government and enforced by the police.

pedestrian A person walking.

right-of-way By law, the right to go first.

text To send a typed message using a cell phone.

READ MORE

Donahue, Jill. L. Ride Right: Bicycle Safety. Minneapolis: Picture Window Books, 2009.

Gibbons, Gail. Bicycle Book. New York: Scholastic, 2001.

Herrington, Lisa M. Bicycle Safety. New York: Children's Press, 2012.

Mara, Wil. What Should I Do? On my Bike. Ann Arbor, Mich.: Cherry Lake, 2012.

WEBSITES

BICYCLE HELMET VIDEOS
http://www.helmets.org/videos.htm
Learn how to properly fit your bike helmet.

KIDS HEALTH: BIKE SAFETY
http://kidshealth.org/kid/watch/out/bike_safety.html
Read more about bike safety for kids.

SAFETY FOR KIDS | KIDS.GOV
http://kids.usagov/health-and-safety/safety/index.shtml
This site has information on many safety topics, including bicycle safety.

Every effort has been made to ensure that these websites are appropriate for children. However, because of the nature of the Internet, it is impossible to guarantee that these sites will remain active indefinitely or that their contents will not be altered.